Merry Christmas —
Brent – Chris – Curt

STRANGE BUT TRUE HOCKEY STORIES

from Bobba 1973

Eighteen stories about some of
hockey's weirdest moments
and zaniest people.

STRANGE BUT TRUE HOCKEY STORIES

by Howard Liss

Illustrated with photographs

PRO HOCKEY
LIBRARY

Random House · New York

PHOTOGRAPH CREDITS: Hockey Hall of Fame, Frank Lennon, 17, 88–89; Pictorial Parade, 34, 41, 44; United Press International, endpapers, 2, 19, 42, 48, 49, 68, 70, 78–79, 100–101, 114 (bottom), 115, 138–139; Wide World, 10, 25, 30, 61, 76, 84, 93, 95, 104, 108, 113, 114 (top), 118–119, 130, 142, 144. Cover art by Ed Vebell.

Manufactured in the United States of America

Library of Congress Cataloging in Publication Data

Liss, Howard.
    Strange but true hockey stories.
    (Pro hockey library [no. 3])
    SUMMARY: Retells unusual events in the history of hockey.
    1. Hockey—Juvenile literature. [1. Hockey]
I. Title.
GV847.25.L5   796.9′62   72-719
ISBN 0-394-82463-6
ISBN 0-394-92463-0 (lib. bdg.)

For Joshua Weisser,
a great hockey fan

CONTENTS

INTRODUCTION

Strange things have happened in all sports and hockey is no exception. In fact some of the strangest incidents could have happened only in hockey.

In its early years, hockey was played with a hard rubber lacrosse ball. One day, according to hockey legend, the players banged the ball so hard that it bounced all over the arena, smashing about $300 worth of windows. In desperation the proprietor seized the ball and sliced off two sections of the sphere, leaving a circular disc, flat on two sides. And that was how the hockey puck was born.

Before the turn of the century, hockey rinks were usually decorated with flags hanging from the rafters. In one game a player took a shot but popped the puck high into the air. For a few seconds nobody knew where it had gone. A luckless goalie soon found out—the hard way. The puck had become tangled in a Canadian Union Jack above the goalie. It finally fell, bounced off the goalie's back and rolled into the net for a goal!

Hockey *is* like other sports in one important way

Conn Smythe.

—psychology. A team's attitude plays an important role in determining the outcome of a game. Conn Smythe, owner of the Toronto Maple Leafs, was a master at psyching up his team.

Toronto faced Montreal in the 1947 Stanley Cup finals. Before the first game Smythe gave his players a pep talk. He wanted them to realize how important it was to get off on the right foot by winning the opening match. This time the pep talk didn't work. His overconfident team was trounced 6-0.

Smythe decided that he had used psychology once too often. He decided not to say another word during the series. This touch of *reverse* psychology paid off. The players responded by knocking off the Canadiens in six games to win the title.

Smythe followed up his silence with another strange strategy. The sixth game of the final series was to be played in Toronto and the Leafs would be champions if they won. Smythe should have had the Stanley Cup brought to Toronto so that it could be presented to the Leafs if the game was a victory.

But the wily Leaf coach remembered how overconfident his team had been before the first game of the series. He was afraid that they would become overconfident again if they learned that the Cup had been brought to Toronto.

The Maple Leafs won the game—Conn Smythe's trick had worked. But when the time came for the team to be presented the Stanley Cup, it was nowhere to be found. It was still on display in a store window in Montreal.

There are so many strange but true hockey stories that they could not all fit in one book. On the pages that follow there is only a sampling of them. Some are well known, some are obscure. But they are all strange—and they are all true.

STRANGE BUT TRUE HOCKEY STORIES

SHORT-HANDED VICTORY

In one way hockey is different from any other major sport. In baseball, football and basketball, the teams always match up man-against-man. But a hockey team can be outnumbered. When a player is penalized, he is sent out of the game for at least two minutes and he cannot be replaced. That's when the going gets tough. The pressure is especially heavy in a Stanley Cup playoff, when one goal may decide a championship. When a team in the playoffs is short-handed, it usually feels it has been successful if the other team fails to score. But the 1928 New York Rangers won a Stanley Cup while short-handed.

The Rangers breezed through the Stanley Cup semifinals, beating Pittsburgh and Boston. But they knew the finals would not be so easy. First, they faced the Montreal Maroons, a great team. Montreal was led by the fearsome "S Line"—forwards Nels Stewart, Hooley Smith and Babe Siebert. But to make things even more difficult, Madison Square Garden, the Rangers' home ice, was unavailable. All games in the best three-out-of-five series would have to be played at Montreal's Forum. Since it's well known that the home team always has a slight advantage, the Rangers' prospects were dim.

Montreal opened strongly, scoring a 2-0 victory in the first game. The second game was a different story, however, and its drama has become part of hockey legend.

Lorne Chabot, the Ranger goalie, was struck over

the left eye by a flying puck and had to leave the game. Coach Lester Patrick had no one to take Chabot's place, so he asked to borrow a goalie from another team. The Maroons, however, insisted that only a member of the Ranger squad could appear on the ice. So the 45-year-old Patrick donned the pads himself, guarding the net for the rest of the game and even into overtime. The Rangers won, 2-1, on Frankie Boucher's goal.

Lester Patrick substitutes for the injured goalie.

For the third game Montreal allowed the Rangers to use Joe Miller, a goalie who had played for the New York Americans. The Americans weren't a winning team with Miller and the Rangers didn't win with him either. Once again the New Yorkers were blanked 2-0. One more victory for the Maroons and they would win the Stanley Cup.

But the Rangers refused to die. Goalie Chabot returned for the fourth game and closed the door on the Maroons. It was a tight game, just as the first three had been. Only one goal was scored all night— by the Rangers' Frankie Boucher, who had pushed home the winning goal in the second game. Now the series was tied at two victories apiece.

The Rangers were under terrific pressure. Playing before fans who rooted against them hurt their morale. And scoring was difficult, just as they figured it would be.

The fifth and last game seemed to turn against them early when one Ranger was sent off the ice with a penalty. The Maroons swept down the ice against the undermanned Ranger defense, passing the puck around and setting up for a shot.

Suddenly Boucher broke in and stole the rubber. He took off swiftly, with only one defenseman, Red Dutton, in front of him. Boucher never broke his stride. He poked the puck through Dutton's legs, went around him, regained possession and cracked the puck past goalie Clint Benedict.

Years after his Stanley Cup heroics, Boucher (right) wins the Cup again as Ranger coach in 1940.

The Maroons fought back savagely while the Rangers tried desperately to fight them off. With the score tied 1-1, the New York team found itself short-handed once again. And once again Frankie Boucher got possession of the puck.

The Ranger center got control of the rubber at center ice. Thinking quickly, he shot the puck to the boards, hoping to control his own rebound. But Boucher figured the angle wrong and the puck skittered ahead.

Maroon defenseman Dunc Monro started to go for the rubber. So did Boucher. Then Monro hesitated, thinking he couldn't beat Boucher to the puck. Boucher kept going and got there first. There was no one in front of him except goalie Clint Benedict. Boucher drove and slammed the puck at the goal. The Montreal goalie dived desperately but missed. Boucher had scored again.

Lorne Chabot stopped Montreal's shots the rest of the way and the Rangers won 2-1, taking the Stanley Cup back to New York.

It was a strange, truly amazing victory for the Rangers. They had overcome all sorts of obstacles. They played the entire series away from home. In the third game a 45-year-old coach replaced an injured goalie.

But most amazing of all was the performance of Frankie Boucher. His overtime goal won the second game and tied the series. By scoring the only goal in the fourth game, he won a second contest and tied the series again.

In the last game Boucher scored both Ranger goals without assistance. And both times he scored when the Rangers had only five men on the ice. He won the Stanley Cup, scoring two single-handed goals for a short-handed team.

WHAT'S IN A NAME?

Most forward lines in hockey work best as units. The center and two wingmen that make up a front line spend hours practicing together, and they know each other's tricks, moves and habits.

Once a front line shows it can score and win for a team, it usually gets a nickname. Often a sportswriter or the team's public relations man creates a name for it, and the public soon picks it up. In the history of hockey there have been many great front lines with catchy nicknames.

In the 1920s the Montreal Maroons had a fine front line consisting of Nels Stewart, Hooley Smith and Babe Siebert. Since their names all began with the same letter, they were called the "S Line."

In the 1930s Conn Smythe's Maple Leafs had a magnificent young unit made up of Charlie Conacher, Harvey "Busher" Jackson and "Gentleman Joe" Primeau. Because of their youth they were nicknamed the "Kid Line."

The Montreal Canadiens of the 1940s had great talent in their "Punch Line"—Elmer Lach, Toe Blake and Maurice "Rocket" Richard. And the Detroit Red Wings iced a strong scoring threat in their "Production Line"—Gordie Howe, Sid Abel and Ted Lindsay. But the most famous of all was the Boston Bruins' "Kraut Line."

In 1935 a 16-year-old named Milt Schmidt was playing with the Kitchener, Ontario, team. Several NHL clubs had scouted the youngster and then lost interest because Schmidt seemed too light. But Art Ross, the general manager of the Boston Bruins, liked Schmidt's play and invited him to the Boston training camp at St. John, New Brunswick.

Schmidt went to the camp, but he could see that he wasn't ready for the NHL. Ross understood. He patted Schmidt on the back, gave him a new pair of skates and told him to put on some weight before coming back for another tryout with the Bruins.

Schmidt did just that. The following year he returned to the Bruin camp, somewhat heavier and more sure of himself. Two other promising rookies, Bobby Bauer and Woody Dumart, were in camp that year. All three were signed by the Bruins and sent to the Bruin farm team at Providence.

Art Ross had guessed right, not only about Schmidt, but about Dumart and Bauer as well. The three youngsters came up to Boston the next year and almost took the league apart. They powered the Bruins to a first-place finish. Boston lost in the Stanley Cup semi-finals, but they had established themselves as a team to be reckoned with—all because of their new trio.

Boston fans adored Schmidt, Dumart and Bauer. Their names were on the lips of every hockey fan, and indeed they were one of the best forward lines in hockey. Of course they had to have a nickname. And because they all had German names, they were called the "Kraut Line."

In 1938–39 the Kraut Line once again led the Bruins into the playoffs. This time Boston went all the way to the top, defeating the Maple Leafs in five games to win the Stanley Cup. The Bruins took first place again in 1939–40, but they were eliminated by the Rangers in the Stanley Cup playoffs.

By this time the Kraut Line was the finest in the NHL. The trio were heroes wherever they went in Boston. Nothing was too good for them. When Schmidt-Dumart-Bauer took the Bruins to first place and the Stanley Cup again in 1940–41, glasses were raised everywhere in toasts to the great Kraut Line. What fantastic players! How lucky Boston was to have them!

But how quickly things changed!

World War II had begun, and Nazi Germany was seeking world conquest. Canada had been at war since 1939 and the United States joined in the fight in December of 1941. Before long, anyone with a German name was suspected of being a Nazi spy. Even the Kraut Line was suspected.

At first they were booed only on away games. But by the end of the 1941 playoffs, even a few proper Bostonians were muttering about Schmidt, Dumart and Bauer. Their nickname, the Kraut Line, had suddenly become an insult.

By 1942 the booing had become very loud. Boston officials decided that the Kraut Line name had to be changed. Since all three had lived in Kitchener, they were renamed the "Kitchener Kids."

Schmidt, Dumart and Bauer were hurt and bewildered by the jeers of the fans. They were patriotic Canadians. What did it matter that their ancestors were German? Did that make them enemy agents?

The Kitchener Kids led the Bruins to the Stanley Cup playoffs again in 1942, but the team lost. Then, after the season, all three of them enlisted in the Royal Canadian Air Force.

The Kraut Line—Schmidt, Dumart and Bauer—on their way to join the Air Force. Mrs. Bauer and Schmidt's girlfriend are in the background.

After the war, Schmidt, Dumart and Bauer re-joined the Bruins. The boos had long since stopped, and the fans were willing to accept the boys' former nickname, the Kraut Line. One final time the trio took Boston into the Stanley Cup playoffs. But Montreal's Punch Line (Lach-Blake-Richard) stole the show and Boston was eliminated.

The 1946–47 season was the last for the Kraut Line. After the season Bobby Bauer retired, even though he was only 32 years old. Dumart and Schmidt played a few more years and then they too hung up their skates.

There is no doubt that the Kraut Line was one of hockey's greatest. From 1936–37 through 1946–47 (with three years out for service in the RCAF) this fantastic trio scored a total of 807 points, including 374 goals.

The Kraut Line is still remembered fondly in Boston and Milt Schmidt was associated with the Bruins for many years as general manager. But for a few dark years it seemed that these three great players might be hooted out of hockey because they had the wrong kind of last names and the wrong nickname.

HOCKEY'S FASTEST
HAT TRICK

It's not easy for an athlete to get his name in a record book. It usually takes an entire career of outstanding play or a whole season of tremendous effort to set a record. And sooner or later nearly every new mark is broken.

Yet there is an exception to every rule. Bill Mosienko of the Chicago Black Hawks set a record in less time than the average reader will need to read the words on this page. And it is highly unlikely that his record will ever be broken.

"Mosie," as he was often called, was a comparatively small man. He was 5 feet 8 inches tall, and the most he weighed during his career was 160 pounds. Some good judges of hockey talent told him he was too light to withstand the punishment of NHL hockey. They said he would never last in the major league. But Mosienko fooled them all.

Part of Mosienko's success was due to his tremendous speed. Few doubted that he was the fastest man on skates during his time with the Black Hawks. But he was more than just a speedy skater—he was a shooter as well. During his NHL career he scored 258 goals.

One day in March 1952, Mosienko was visiting a friend in Toronto, and the two men spent a couple of hours at their favorite pastime—thumbing through the hockey record book.

"It sure would be nice if I could get my name in there some day," remarked Mosienko.

"Don't worry, Bill," replied his friend. "I'm betting someday it will happen."

Forty-eight hours later Bill's wish came true.

On March 23, 1952, the Hawks played the New York Rangers. It hadn't been a good season for either team. Neither club had qualified for the playoffs. Thus it was just another game. There would be lots of action, but the contest itself had no bearing on the league standings.

During the swirl of play, Chicago's center, Gus Bodnar, gained possession of the puck. Mosienko broke through the Ranger defense, and Bodnar shot him an accurate pass. Mosienko picked up the puck and fired. Goal!

Next came the face-off at center ice. Bodnar gained control of the puck and flicked a quick pass to Mosienko, who zoomed in on the net and shot. Goal again!

The teams came back to center ice for another face-off. Again Bodnar took the rubber away. This time he passed to left winger George Gee while Mosienko went down the ice on the right. Gee saw his teammate open and fed him the puck. Mosie swished his stick once more. Goal number three!

As the stunned Rangers skated silently back to their positions, it was announced that a new record had been set.

Bill Mosienko had scored three goals in exactly *21 seconds*!

Hockey experts soon discovered some startling facts about Mosienko's new mark. Previously, the fastest three goals had been scored in 24 seconds. But that was a *team* record, set by the Montreal Maroons in 1932. Three different players had scored those goals: Hooley Smith, Babe Siebert and Dave Trottier.

The record for the fastest one-man hat trick had been held by Carl Liscombe of the Detroit Red Wings. He scored his trio of markers in 64 seconds.

Strangely enough, Liscombe had set his record against the Chicago Black Hawks in 1938. It had taken a Chicago player—Bill Mosienko—to improve on that mark.

In a game where a team rarely scores more than five goals in sixty minutes, the chances of one man scoring three goals in a fraction of a minute are slim indeed. The lucky man who did it got his name in the record book in record time—and his accomplishment is so unlikely that his name may stay in the record book forever.

Amazing Bill Mosienko scores his third goal in 21 seconds of play.

THE VOICE OF HOCKEY

On the afternoon of March 22, 1923, the radio editor of the Toronto *Daily Star* called an 18-year-old cub reporter into his office.

"I have a special assignment for you," he told the young newsman. "You're going to broadcast a hockey game tonight, between Parkdale and the Kitchener Seniors."

Broadcasting a hockey game was a new idea—in fact, it had never been tried before. But the reporter was tired. He had been on the go since seven o'clock that morning, and the thought of working at night was almost too much. "Why can't you give the job to someone in the sports department?" he asked.

"Because you've had some radio experience," replied the editor. "Besides, I know you can handle it."

Wearily the reporter made his way to the Mutual Street Arena where the game was to be played. He munched a hot dog, and then helped set up his broadcast "booth," which turned out to be a glass enclosure situated near the penalty bench. It was four feet square and four feet high. The only equipment he had was a milking stool with sawed-off legs and a telephone. To get on the air he telephoned the engineer at radio station CFCA, which was owned by the newspaper. The reporter spoke into the telephone and his words were relayed by the station's transmitter.

Alone in his cramped quarters, with no one to re-

Broadcaster Foster Hewitt (right), Canada's voice of hockey, with his son William, who took over when his father retired.

lieve him, the young sportscaster suffered through a rough night. Because the stool was so small, his knees were practically up to his chin. The booth was closed to keep out the crowd noises, and it got stuffy and damp in the enclosure. Vapor misted over the glass so that he could barely make out the figures of the players. They seemed to be skating in a fog as they flashed around the ice. To add to his misery, the game went into three overtime periods.

But he kept talking throughout the game and the intermissions. When it was all over, the reporter found that he had broadcast non-stop for three solid hours!

There weren't many radio sets in Canada in 1923, but the station's few listeners were delighted with the hockey broadcast. They demanded more. Since the newspaper was anxious to please its customers, hockey soon became a regular radio event.

Not only was the cub reporter the first man to broadcast a hockey game, but in time he became the most famous sportscaster in Canada. The young man's name was Foster Hewitt.

Actually, Hewitt had little experience when he first announced a hockey game. About a year before, he had visited a radio show in Detroit. At that time some people still didn't know what a radio was. They couldn't understand how a human voice could cross miles of open air and come out through a loudspeaker. The special program in Detroit featured baseball's Ty Cobb and other celebrities. Hewitt was so impressed that he persuaded a manufacturer to allow him to sell their radios in Canada. Later, he took a job with another company and helped manufacture radios.

When he heard that the Toronto *Star* was about to own a station, Foster Hewitt determined to get in "on the ground floor." His father was sports editor of the *Star* and soon young Foster was on the staff as a reporter. He gathered news for the paper, but he also did some spot radio announcing, giving the titles and composers of music played during radio concerts.

He also had some peculiar radio assignments. The *Star* had purchased a truck and installed a radio receiver. Hewitt's job was to drive the truck to beaches, fairs and parks. There he would turn up the volume, and give free radio shows to groups of astonished listeners. Finally, in March of 1923, he announced the hockey game.

Hewitt later broadcast some baseball and football games and wrote about radio for the newspaper. He also became an on-the-spot announcer at special events. But he was destined to earn his reputation as a hockey sportscaster.

In 1931 he got his big break. Conn Smythe had just completed his Maple Leaf Gardens and he realized how radio broadcasts could increase interest in his team. He asked Hewitt to broadcast the games of the Toronto Maple Leafs.

Some sports announcers in the United States became famous in the 1930s and 1940s. But none of them approached the fame and popularity of Foster Hewitt in Canada. His tense, high-pitched voice was imitated by thousand of fans, who loved to use Hewitt's favorite phrase, "He shoots—he scores!" When he was broadcasting a crucial game, normal life in Canada came to a standstill as fans throughout the country sat near their radio sets.

Hewitt got fan mail from trading posts on Hudson Bay, from fishing trawlers in the North Atlantic, from northern lumber camps and solitary lighthouses. In 1937 one important game between Detroit and Toronto was heard by six million people.

Hewitt often insisted that his listeners were interested only in the excitement of a hockey game, not in Foster Hewitt personally. But he was wrong about that. Did Hewitt have a cold and his voice sound raspy? The mails brought a torrent of cough syrups, cough drops and a thousand home-cure remedies. Once he broadcast while wearing a derby; the Leafs were losing, and Hewitt suggested to his listeners that his derby might be bringing Toronto bad luck. Then he announced that he was removing it from his head. Suddenly the Leafs went on a scoring spree and they pulled the game out of the fire. In a matter of days Hewitt had received hat-hangers of all shapes and sizes, with instructions to keep his hat off during the game.

He also received thousands of letters, cards and gifts from his admirers. They sent him cakes, clothing, walking sticks, cigarettes, homemade candy. On his birthday the mailman would stagger in with sacks full of greeting cards.

So great was Foster Hewitt's popularity that during World War II the Canadian government broadcast his descriptions of games to the Canadian soldiers overseas. The Germans even tried to use those broadcasts for their own advantage. They rebroadcast Hewitt's accounts of games, adding the voice of a young woman during intermissions. Playing on the soldiers' homesickness, she suggested that they stop fighting and go home so that they could hear hockey and Foster Hewitt all the time.

In any sport, the Hall of Fame is reserved for the greatest players, or those who have made a lasting contribution to the game. For his services as a pioneer in hockey broadcasting, Foster Hewitt was elected to the Hockey Hall of Fame. To every old-time fan who ever listened to his thrilling account of the action down below, Foster Hewitt will always be "The Voice of Hockey."

THE MAGIC NUMBER

There is one record in sports that most sports fans know instantly—Babe Ruth's career home run total of 714.

In the years since the Babe set that record in 1935, 714 has become a "magic number." It is a symbol of excellence, not only for baseball but for many sports. In hockey a career total of 714 goals would be a monumental feat. A man would have to score 50 goals a season for 14 seasons to even come close.

Maurice "Rocket" Richard set an amazing record of his own for career goals in hockey, banging in 544 in 18 seasons. When he retired in 1960 after 978 games, not counting playoff matches, his 544 was the mark to beat in hockey. No one dreamed that a hockey player would approach 714.

On October 16, 1946, an 18-year-old Detroit wingman named Gordon Howe scored his first National Hockey League goal. The marker came at 13:39 of the second period, and Howe was assisted by Sid Abel and Adam Brown. Nobody took much notice of this one goal then or later, especially since Gordie scored only 7 goals in 50 games that season.

The years went by and Gordie Howe added steadily to his goal total. Some seasons were truly spectacular. In 1950–51 he poked in 43 goals; the next year he had 47; and the year after that he scored 49. In three seasons Howe totaled 139 goals.

Howe had begun his NHL career three years after

Richard. When the Rocket retired in 1960, Howe had 446 goals and had been in the league for 15 years. He needed 98 goals to tie the Rocket, and 99 to go ahead.

It didn't seem likely that Howe could overtake Richard. He hadn't been scoring as much as before —32 goals in 1958–59, and "only" 28 the year Rocket retired. The following season he produced one of his lowest totals, 23 goals.

Like all hockey players, he had taken a terrific beating. Over the years he had suffered numerous broken bones, cuts, bruises and bumps. Gordie seemed to be slowing up and there was some talk of

Long-time scoring champion Maurice Richard scores a goal.

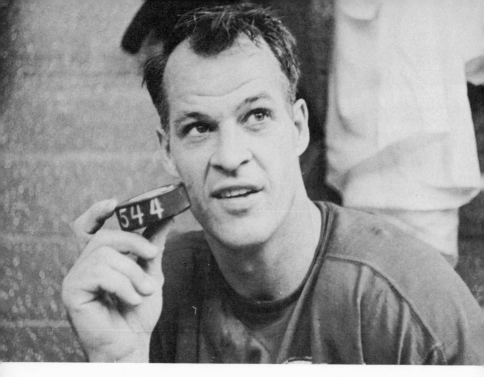

Gordie Howe poses with the puck that scored his 544th goal, tying Richard's lifetime regular-season record.

dropping him back to the defensive line, where he would help the team but wouldn't do much scoring.

Suddenly things changed. In 1961–62 he hiked up his scoring to 33 goals, placing second only to Bobby Hull. The next year he had 38 goals, leading the league. Now Richard's record was within reach.

On October 27, 1963, the Red Wings took the ice against the Montreal Canadiens. And at 11:04 of the third period, with Bill Gadsby and Bruce Mac-Gregor assisting on a power play, Gordie Howe slammed the puck past goalie Gump Worsley to tie Richard's record of 544 goals.

For the next five games Gordie drew a blank. The Red Wings slumped too, losing three of those five games. Then on November 10, the Red Wings took on the Canadiens again, in Detroit.

Olympia Stadium, the Red Wings' home ice, has 12,500 seats. But for this Canadien–Red Wing game 15,027 people shoe-horned their way in, many sitting in the aisles or standing in the back. They had come for one big reason: to see Gordie Howe break the record. He didn't disappoint them.

Detroit was leading 2-0 when Alex Faulkner committed a major penalty and went off the ice. Howe and Billy McNeill came in as penalty-killers.

Gordie got the puck off the boards and passed to McNeill, and the two Red Wings drove across the blue line. Hemmed in, McNeill passed back to Gordie, who moved to the face-off circle at center ice and whacked a shot to goalie Charlie Hodges' left. The puck skimmed past the post and zinged into the net. The crowd at the Olympia cheered wildly as Gordie raised his stick high in triumph. For ten minutes the fans cheered and applauded, showering the ice with hats, cushions and assorted junk.

Gordie Howe continued to play, and the records continued to fall. On November 27, 1965, he scored his 600th regular-season goal, and on December 4, 1968, he registered number 700.

On February 6, 1969, the Red Wings went up against the Chicago Black Hawks. At 12:47 of the

first period Howe took a pass from Alex Delvecchio, bored in on goalie Dave Dryden and scored.

It was goal number 714! Then he scored two more goals before the game was over.

They cheered Gordie for his goals, just as they did any time he scored. But it was only later that people realized Howe had surpassed Babe Ruth's magic number. Dozens of newspaper columns were written about the feat. The remarkable Gordie Howe had passed 714. How many would he score before he hung up his skates?

On April 3, 1971, Howe scored his final goal in a game against the Chicago Black Hawks. Shortly afterward, after 25 years of stardom, he retired. In regular-season play he had scored 786 goals.

Records are made to be broken. Babe Ruth's home run record and Howe's goal record may both be broken in time. But some records are more impressive than others. Even after new marks have been set, baseball's 714 and hockey's 786 will be remembered as tributes to the legendary men who accomplished them. They are sports' magic numbers.

Howe in action in 1965 as he approaches his 600th goal.

THE SEASON OF DISASTER

During the 1941–42 season the New York Rangers had finished in first place. In part that was due to the great performance of Grant Warwick, who had won the Calder Trophy as Rookie of the Year.

America entered World War II during that hockey season. The following year a few Rangers were drafted into the army, and a few others were injured. New York finished last in 1942–43. Yet the team shrugged it off. Other clubs had lost players to the draft and suffered injuries. Everything was sure to even up in the end. Next year was sure to be better, especially since there were still some experienced players on the roster, including Warwick, Ott Heller, and the great veteran Bryan Hextall.

But even before the 1943–44 season started, things started to go against the Rangers. Because of wartime restrictions, some Canadian hockey players were not allowed to leave Canada to play with an American team. Thus Dutch Hiller and Phil Watson, two fine skaters, could not join the Rangers for the 1943–44 season.

Any hopes the Rangers had for a better year were quickly dashed once the season started. They lost the opening game 5-2 to Toronto, then were trounced 8-3 by Detroit. Then came losses to Montreal and Chicago. Next it was Toronto again; the Leafs scored four goals in the first period and coasted home, winning 7-4.

Ranger coach Frank Boucher was over 40 years

old and not in the best of condition. But he was desperate for a victory. He reactivated himself, hoping to add extra strength to the team.

In the next game the Rangers faced Boston, the only team they had not lost to. They piled up a 2-0 lead, but blew it and lost 6-2. Next game, Chicago scored 8 goals in the last two periods to beat the Rangers 10-5. Then Detroit beat New York 3-1, Montreal beat New York 5-2, and Boston beat New York 6-2.

The Rangers had played ten games and lost ten

In 1940 (left) the Rangers are in a gay mood after an undefeated streak of 18 games. In 1943, on the brink of the worst season ever, they look more solemn.

games. And during this famine some peculiar things had happened. In a game against Chicago, New York had scored 33 seconds after the opening face-off; and against Detroit, New York had scored after 29 seconds. Surely such quick scores should have lifted Ranger morale. Unfortunately, they didn't. In fact the New Yorkers lost most of their games by at least three goals.

The Rangers hoped to improve matters through a

few trades. From Toronto came Bucko McDonald; and from Boston came a whole new line, consisting of Oscar Aubuchon, Ab DeMarko and Chuck Sherza. In return, New York gave up Red Garrett, Gordie Bell and Chuck Rayner. All three were unavailable at the time, since they were serving in the Canadian navy. So the Rangers got three active players for three inactive players.

After their eleventh loss, to the Canadiens, the Rangers suddenly gained a moral victory—a 2-2 tie with Montreal! We're on our way at last, cheered New York fans. But the hurrahs faded quickly as New York lost its next two games, to Montreal and Chicago.

The poor New Yorkers got two players "on loan" from Montreal, but that didn't help either. In the next game they lost to Boston 9-6. In 15 games they had lost 14 and tied one.

On Sunday, December 12, 1943, the Rangers finally broke the ice. With a 6-4 victory over the Boston Bruins, New York won its first game of the season.

The Rangers didn't stop there, though. They won their very next game, 6-2, over Detroit. Two in a row!

Unfortunately, their victory streak was soon broken. In the return match Detroit won 5-3. Would the sun never shine on the Rangers?

Never say die! cried the Rangers. On Christmas

night they presented their fans with a 5-3 victory over the Maple Leafs. Then they beat Chicago 7-6. A miracle! The Rangers had four wins in five games.

Then the losses started all over again. More players joined the Rangers, but nothing seemed to help. The New York front office needed a revolving door to keep up with players coming and players going.

The Rangers never pulled out of their downward plunge. In short, the 1943–44 season was a disaster. In their remaining 30 games they won only 2, lost 24 and tied 4. Naturally, some records were set—all the wrong kinds of records.

The New York Rangers had the lowest number of victories in a season in National Hockey League history. They won only 6 games, lost 39 and tied 5.

The Rangers also accumulated the lowest number of points in a season in NHL history—17. They trailed the next lowest team, Boston, by 26 points.

There is a saying in professional athletics: "On any given day, even the last-place team can beat the team in first place." The New York Rangers of 1943–44 almost proved the saying wrong.

ONE-MAN TEAM

The National Hockey League does not keep official records of player height and weight. If records were available, one candidate for "smallest defenseman" would be Francis Michael "King" Clancy.

When Clancy tried out with the Ottawa Senators in 1921 he was barely 18 years old. Skinny and spindly-legged, he stood a mere 5-foot-7 and weighed 130 pounds. It was comical enough that such a stripling wanted to play defense; but considering the team he wanted to join, it was positively outlandish!

Clancy was trying to crack probably the best lineup of players hockey had ever seen. Many were future Hall-of-Famers.

At center for the Senators was Frankie Nighbor, "The Pembroke Peach." It is doubtful that anyone on skates had slicker moves, or was a better passer, playmaker or stickhandler. Opposing players said that he could play an entire game wearing a full-dress suit and never lose the crease in his pants.

Cy Denneny was at left wing. Cy's lifetime record of 246 goals in 334 games places him second in the all-time standings of goals scored per game.

Other all-stars on the club included Punch Broadbent at left wing, Eddie Gerard and Buck Boucher on defense, and Clint Benedict as goaltender.

But Clancy simply wouldn't quit. The youngster kept showing up for practice whether he was asked to come or not. Perhaps it was because he loved hockey so much. Or maybe it was because he didn't dare go home a failure. Clancy's father (also nick-named "King") had been an outstanding Canadian football player, and the son may have felt he had to live up to his dad's athletic reputation.

Ottawa manager Tommy Gorman saw that the teen-ager was full of hustle and that he might even develop into a first-class player some day. Besides, the older players took heart watching Clancy work so hard, and they put out an extra effort to keep up with him. Clancy stuck with the Senators, and on March 31, 1923, he proved his greatness.

The Ottawa Senators qualified for the Stanley Cup playoffs in 1923. The Senators took on the Vancouver club in the semi-finals and polished them off. Next, in the best-of-three games finals, they faced the Edmonton Eskimos, champions of the Western Canada Hockey League. The Senators eked out a 2-1 decision in the first game. But it was clear that the Eskimos were not going to be eliminated without a fight.

The final match proved to be the toughest of the series. The Senators were a tired, hurting team, with only eight men available for duty. One of them was King Clancy.

In the early part of the game, defenseman Eddie Gerard was hurt. As he left the ice Gerard yelled, "Get in there, Clancy!"

Clancy went out on defense, zigzagging all over the rink and thwarting the Eskimo attack. Gerard felt better after a while and came back in. Clancy left the ice.

He was back a few minutes later to replace Buck Boucher, who had been checked hard. Once more the twenty-year-old filled in beautifully on defense until Boucher recovered.

In the second period it was Frankie Nighbor's turn to take a beating. As he came out wheezing, King Clancy took over, this time at center. And although he played more like a defenseman than a forward, he did a good job. He kept the Eskimos from setting up a sustained drive, stopping their attack in their own territory.

Nighbor came back in, and Clancy was out—but not for long. Cy Denneny was cut by a stick and had to leave the ice. Clancy went in at left wing this time. And again he left the game when Denneny was ready to return. But he wasn't finished by a long shot.

Punch Broadbent was puffing and panting in total exhaustion. So Clancy replaced him at right wing.

The game went into the final minutes with Ottawa clinging desperately to a 1-0 lead. If they could hold that lead, they would win the Cup two games to none.

Then goalie Clint Benedict drew a two-minute penalty for slashing. As he left he tossed his big-bladed stick to Clancy. "Here, kid," he called out. "Take care of this place till I get back."

Clancy had never played goalie in his life. He also wore no pads. But he guarded the net fearlessly, inspiring his teammates to greater effort. They harassed the Eskimos constantly and kept them from shooting. As the two-minute penalty was ending, Clancy shot out of the net, took the puck, skated down the ice and shot. It didn't go in, and Clancy skated back quickly. A few seconds later Benedict returned, smiling, to take over in the goal for Clancy.

Finally, the game was over, and the Ottawa Senators had won 1-0. The Stanley Cup was theirs.

Perhaps some other NHL skater has played *all six positions* in a single playoff game, but there is no record of it. Francis Michael "King" Clancy did, and against many odds—including his size. Hockey's "shrimp" had shown the best of them what it takes to be a champion.

FATHER AND SON

Parry Sound is a small town about 100 miles north of Toronto. It gets mighty cold up there. Frigid winds whip down on Parry Sound from Georgian Bay, a body of water connected to Lake Huron. The ice starts forming along the shore and on rivers and streams late in November or early December, and it doesn't break up until April.

Hockey scouts have learned that many good prospects come from faraway places like Parry Sound. Kids start skating soon after they learn to walk, and more often than not they are carrying hockey sticks. Scouts trek out to places like Parry Sound because they know that they may discover a great hockey player. Such players as Gordie Howe, Alex Delvecchio and Jean Beliveau came from the far reaches of the Canadian north.

In 1942 Harold "Baldy" Cotton, chief scout of the Boston Bruins, heard about a couple of good young players in Western Ontario named Pete Horeck and Doug Orr. Cotton went to see them play and was quite impressed. Horeck looked good, but Orr looked even better. He was a faster skater, a better stick handler, and he was bigger and stronger than Horeck. Cotton wanted them both to try out with a Boston farm team.

Horeck agreed, but Doug Orr had other plans. World War II had broken out and he wanted to enlist in the navy. So Horeck reported to the Atlantic City Seagulls of the Eastern Hockey League, and

Doug Orr joined the navy.

Over the years Pete Horeck advanced to Cleveland of the American Hockey League and then to the NHL, playing for several years with Chicago, Detroit and Boston. Doug Orr could probably have had an even better hockey career. But when the war ended and Orr returned home, he had new responsibilities. He had a wife and a growing family to support. At 21, he felt he was too old to begin a hockey career. Instead, he got a job and settled down in Parry Sound.

On March 20, 1948, the Orrs' third child, Robert, was born. There were some complications at first, and for a few hours it was feared that the infant might not live. But in a day or two Bobby was out of danger.

Doug Orr knew the game of hockey thoroughly, and when Bobby was only five years old Doug was already teaching him the basics of the game. The boy was small but he was already quick and sure. Bobby began to play organized hockey at the Parry Sound Community Center. He started with the Minor Squirt Division, then progressed through Squirts, PeeWees and Bantams. He was soon placed ahead of his age group because he was too good for boys his own age.

In 1960 a group of officials with the Boston Bruins journeyed to Gananoque, 300 miles east of Parry Sound, to see the all-Ontario Bantam championship.

The Bruin scouts were experienced hockey men—
Milt Schmidt (a former Bruin all-star), Lynn Patrick
(a member of the "Royal Patrick Family") and Wren
Blair (coach of the Kingston Frontenacs, a Boston
farm team). By the end of the first period they were
staring at 12-year-old defenseman Bobby Orr.

"Incredible!" said Schmidt. "The way that boy
skates without wasted motion. Reminds me of Doug
Harvey!"

"No, no," Lynn Patrick disagreed. "He's more like
Eddie Shore—he keeps the puck in front of him, always looking for an opening."

Orr did everything well. The Bruin scouts agreed:
this was one boy the Bruins *had* to have.

The Boston officials decided to play it cool. They
did not want to move too quickly and tip off the
other NHL teams. After all, Bobby wasn't even a
teen-ager yet, and if the word spread about him,
there would be plenty of time for some other club to
grab him.

Cautiously, they asked if a major league team was
sponsoring the Parry Sound teams. The answer was
no. The Bruins gladly put up $1,000 a year for three
years to support the teams. Sponsoring the teams
gave Boston the right to deal with any Parry Sound
player first. According to the rules, a team could gain
rights to a player when he turned 14. Of course the
Bruins wanted Bobby, and they intended to sign him
to a Junior A card on his 14th birthday.

Other NHL teams found out about Bobby, and in the next two years a number of them approached the Orrs with deals. Doug Orr was a Toronto fan and

Boston rookie Bobby Orr leaves the hospital after an injury.

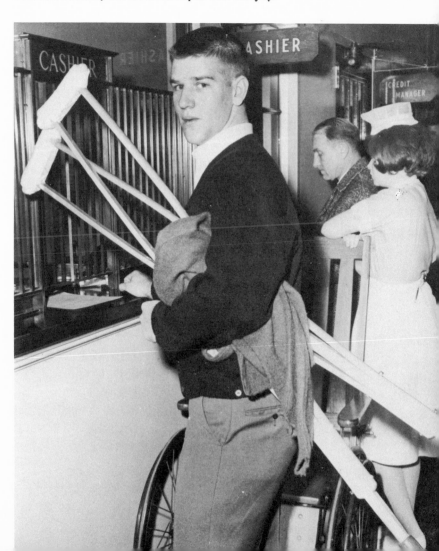

might have signed Bobby with the Maple Leafs. But the Toronto scout went around Doug Orr, trying to gain the support of Bobby's school principal. Doug didn't like that.

In 1962, when Bobby was 14, the Bruins invited him to their training camp at Niagara Falls. When he arrived, there were enough prospects for a dozen full teams. But after the first few days of practice it was obvious that Orr was far better than anyone there.

Of course Bobby eventually signed with Boston, and the rest of his story is well known. In his first five years of play he won just about every award in sight, including the Calder Memorial Trophy as rookie of the year; the James Norris Memorial Trophy as best defenseman of the year; the Art Ross Memorial Trophy as the scoring champion of the NHL; the Conn Smythe Memorial Trophy as most valuable player to his team in the Stanley Cup playoffs; the Hart Memorial Trophy as most valuable player in the regular season; and the Lou Marsh Trophy as the top Canadian athlete of the year.

No one doubts that Bobby Orr was the most spectacular player in a generation. But luck may have played its part in his success. Some sportswriters think that if Doug Orr had played big league hockey, no one would ever have heard of Bobby Orr.

If Doug had accepted Baldy Cotton's offer of a tryout with Boston, he would have become a Bruin and Bobby might have grown up in Boston instead of Parry Sound. Bobby would have had fewer opportunities to skate and perhaps less encouragement from his father. In fact, he might not have been a hockey player at all.

Many NHL players fervently wish he *had* done something else—anything else besides hockey.

HOCKEY'S ZANIEST TEAM

Hockey is fast, dangerous and full of hard action. From the opening face-off to the final buzzer the players skate through a hail of flying pucks. They get poked by sticks, slammed to the boards, tripped, elbowed and shoved. It is not surprising that when they are on the ice, hockey players have quick tempers.

But when the game is over the players relax. Some of them ease the tension by playing practical jokes on their teammates, and they are like gleeful children when their pranks work well. One team full of practical jokers was the Toronto Maple Leafs of the 1930s. The Toronto club had some of the great names in hockey, but many of them might have earned their livings as clowns or comedians. Among the zanies were Charlie Conacher, Hap Day, King Clancy and Red Horner. Some of their capers have become hockey legends.

One of their special targets was teammate Baldy Cotton, a great stickhandler and an expert at "ragging the puck." When the team was short-handed because a player had been penalized and sent off the ice, Baldy took over. Along with Joe Primeau and one or two others, he would zig and zag and pass the puck back and forth until the penalty time was over.

Baldy had one weakness—clothes. He fancied himself the best dresser in hockey. When a new style came into fashion, Baldy was the first to try it. He was proud of his clothes—almost vain.

When derby hats came into fashion, Baldy soon bought one. He wore it at a rakish angle and boasted that it suited him well. His teammates put up with his vanity awhile. Then Charlie Conacher decided to teach Baldy a lesson in humility.

The Leafs boarded a train for New York City, where they were to play the Rangers. Some of the players, including Conacher, settled down to a game of cards in the club car. Baldy carefully hung his new derby on a peg and watched the game. A few minutes later Conacher excused himself. On his way out of the car he lifted the derby and took it with him.

Conacher returned a few minutes later with a black derby jammed down to his ears. "Hey, Baldy," he called out, "how does this thing look on me?"

Conacher's head was much larger than Cotton's and the hat was obviously stretched. "You big ape, stop clowning!" screamed Baldy. "Take that hat off before you pull it out of shape!"

"Take it easy," Conacher replied mildly. He went from one teammate to another, asking how he looked in a black derby. All this time Cotton was complaining and trying to get the hat away from Conacher.

Finally Conacher pretended to be disgusted. He tugged violently at the hat, pulling it off his head and ripping the brim from the crown. Scornfully he tossed the brim to Cotton.

"Take it, Baldy," he growled. "It doesn't look good on me anyway."

"My hat!" groaned Baldy. "It cost fifteen dollars. You ruined it."

At last Conacher decided the joke had gone far enough and he produced Baldy's black derby hat. The Leafs roared with laughter.

The Leafs didn't enjoy visiting Boston very much because they stayed at the University Club, which was full of old retired members. During one stay, Hap Day hit upon an idea for some fun.

Day had an expensive suit that he was proud of. But it had been stained and ruined. Since no one else on the team knew about the damage, Day saw a chance to trick Red Horner. He went to chief prankster Conacher.

"Let's tell Red that for a twenty-five dollar bet, I'll dive into the club's pool with my suit on. That way I can make an easy twenty-five to help pay for a new suit."

Conacher was delighted with the idea. He made the proposition to Horner. But Horner was suspicious. He was a practical joker himself, and he sensed that something funny was going on.

"Red, you can't lose," said Conacher, talking fast. "We tell the guys that you bet Hap twenty-five dollars he wouldn't jump into the pool with his suit on. Then we collect a dollar from each of them to see

the show. It's a good laugh and you don't lose a thing."

Horner finally agreed. Conacher stood at the door while the team trooped into the pool area. Then Hap Day entered, wearing his suit. He solemnly plunged into the pool while the Leafs cheered mightily. Day emerged from the water and collected his bet from Horner.

Horner then turned to Conacher. "Where's the admission money?"

"Golly, Red, I was so excited I forgot about asking them for their dollars," said Conacher, his eyes twinkling. Horner's face dropped and he turned away, realizing he had fallen into the trap set by Day and Conacher.

Although they were pranksters, the Leafs were also a great team. When they tried their next practical joke they were in first place by ten points. This time the victim was coach Dick Irvin.

Before coming to Toronto, Irvin had been fired by the Chicago Black Hawks. He thought he had been treated unfairly and he wanted revenge. So, before the Leafs were to play the Black Hawks, Irvin pushed his players for a big win. He didn't want to win by just one or two goals. He wanted a lopsided score.

Practical joker Charlie Conacher puts on a solemn expression for the camera.

Conacher with teammates Joe Primeau and Harvey "Busher" Jackson.

Perhaps Irvin was too grim. He nagged the Leafs constantly about the Chicago game until it was finally too much to take. Before the game, the players got together for a secret meeting and decided to take things easy during the first part of the contest. Let the Hawks score a couple of goals, they said. *That* would upset Irvin. Then maybe he wouldn't be so anxious next time. Of course, the Leafs were confident they could come back and win later in the game.

However, the joke didn't work out quite as planned. Chicago scored twice in the first period.

During intermission, Irvin was furious. The team chuckled behind his back, thinking that their plan was going well. But in the next period Chicago scored again. Now it was 3-0.

Hap Day was getting worried. "Let's get 'em now," he muttered to his teammates. But it was too late. Chicago held on to its lead, and nothing the Leafs did was enough to win. Day, Conacher and the others didn't dare tell Irvin about their practical joke after it had backfired. Instead, they resolved to make it up to their coach the next time they faced Chicago.

In the rematch the Leafs were a fired-up team. Chicago goalie Charlie Gardiner tried desperately to block the barrage of shots, but it was useless. Toronto kept up the pressure, scoring goal upon goal. One zooming shot hit Gardiner's forehead and he dropped to the ice with blood streaming from the cut.

Substitute goalie Wilf Cude took over but fared no better. In fact, he too was smacked by a shot and had to be helped off the ice. Gardiner returned with his head bandaged to finish the game.

Just before the end of the game, when the final goal was banged in, a joyous fan skimmed his derby onto the ice. Gardiner picked it up and put it on his head. But if he thought it would help, it didn't. A few minutes later Toronto skated off the ice with a resounding 11-1 victory.

There were a couple of screwballs on every team in those days. But none compared with the zanies of Toronto. Hockey players didn't earn as much money then as they do now, but they seem to have had a lot more fun.

THE SHUTOUT
GOALIE

Most players in the NHL begin their careers in their late teens or early twenties. If a player doesn't start early, chances are he will never play in the NHL.

Bill Durnan was different. He broke into the big league when he was 28 years old. And even then he didn't want to become a professional hockey player. But the most remarkable thing about this reluctant late-starter is that he holds one of hockey's most fantastic records.

When he was 14 years old, Durnan began to play organized hockey with the Junior North Torontos of the Ontario Hockey Association. The Toronto Maple Leafs thought that he might develop into a good player, so he was placed on their reserve list. But hockey was not Bill's only talent. He was also considered one of the best young softball players in the area.

One summer Durnan injured his knee wrestling with a friend. He couldn't play hockey the following winter, and the Maple Leafs forgot about him.

Durnan didn't seem to mind. His knee healed, and the next summer he played softball, increasing his reputation as an outstanding pitcher. He played hockey in the winter, first with Sudbury and then as goalie with Kirkland Lake's championship team. After that he hooked on with the Montreal Royals, a Canadiens' amateur farm team. Still, the prospect of playing in the NHL seemed lost to him forever.

In 1943 World War II was raging in Europe and

the Pacific, and many NHL regulars had gone off to fight. One of these was Paul Bibeault, the Canadiens' goaltender. Durnan, who was then 28 years old, had continued playing softball and hockey, but only in his spare time. He had a regular job in the office of a steel company. Nevertheless, when Bibeault left for the war, the Canadiens invited Durnan to try out for the job. Bill refused the offer at first, thinking he was too old to make good in the majors. But Durnan's boss, an avid hockey fan, insisted that he give it a try before deciding he wasn't good enough. Reluctantly, Durnan changed his mind. He made the team and that turned out to be a sad day for the Canadiens' NHL opponents.

In his first year with Montreal, Durnan played in all 50 games and allowed just 109 goals. That season the Canadiens won 38 games, lost only 5 and tied 7. Durnan not only won the Vezina Trophy as best goalie, but was also selected as first-string goalie on the All-Star team!

Old-time hockey fans refused to believe that Durnan was that good. They found all sorts of reasons to put him down. They pointed out that most of the NHL stars were in the armed forces and Durnan didn't have to face them. Besides, the Canadiens' fabulous front line, Toe Blake, Elmer Lach and Rocket Richard (who scored 50 goals in 1943–44), seemed to take charge of the puck in every game. Furthermore, Montreal's excellent defense gave the

Ace goalie Bill Durnan.

rookie goalie plenty of help. Durnan, the "experts" decided, was just lucky.

Durnan proved them wrong. The following year, 1944–45, he duplicated his first-year feat, winning the Vezina Trophy as the NHL's best goalie, and the coveted nomination as first-string goalie on the All-Star team.

When the war ended, many of the hockey greats returned to the ice for the 1945–46 season. Still, Durnan won the Vezina Trophy and the first-string All-Star berth. And even the next year, 1946–47, with the league at full strength, Durnan repeated as the league's best goalie. For four consecutive years Bill Durnan won the Vezina Trophy and was first-string goalie on the All-Star team.

Hockey fans now marveled at his skill. The six-foot, 200-pound goalie played standing up instead of crouching like other goalies, and he depended on his lightning-fast hands. He could often smother shots with his body, or block a sizzler with his stick or skate, but many times he simply caught the rubber in his gloved hand as it whizzed in at him. A hard-shooting forward would boom the puck toward the net, and Big Bill would just reach out with a quick motion and pluck it out of the air. He made it look so easy!

But it wasn't easy. The 1947–48 season was a bad one for Durnan. His knees ached from a painful arthritic condition, and he became nervous and edgy

before games. A hard shot could fracture a man's skull, especially since goalies didn't wear masks in those days. Durnan worried about all this. He felt that he couldn't go on taking the punishment any

Durnan stretches across the ice to make a save.

longer. More than once he told Frank Selke, managing director of the Canadiens, that he wanted to quit. But Selke managed to talk him out of it.

That was fortunate, because in 1948–49 Durnan

was back to his old form. He won the Vezina Trophy for the fifth time in six years. And, of course, he was named top goalie on the All-Star team. But his finest achievement came late in the season.

On February 24, 1949, Montreal played the Black Hawks in Chicago. At 16:15 of the first period, Chicago's Roy Conacher swooped in on Durnan and scored. It was the last Chicago goal of the evening.

Two nights later the Canadiens faced the Detroit Red Wings and Durnan shut them out 1-0. He then blanked the Maple Leafs four nights later as the Canadiens won 2-0. When Durnan got his third shutout in a row against Boston he had gone 223 minutes without allowing a goal. Now he was aiming at the modern record of 290:12, set by Chicago's Charlie Gardiner in 1931.

Next, the Canadiens were scheduled to play the Boston Bruins again. Bill went into the game with confidence, and turned in another shutout, a 1-0 victory. His shutout time was now up to 283 minutes, 45 seconds. He still needed $6\frac{1}{2}$ minutes to break Gardiner's record.

On March 9 Durnan faced the Chicago Black Hawks, the last team to score against him. In the first period he held the Hawks scoreless to set a new shutout record. But at 5:36 of the second period, Black Hawk Gaye Stewart scored, ending the streak.

The magnificent Montreal goalie had gone 309 minutes and 21 seconds without allowing a goal.

In 1949–50 Durnan won the Vezina Trophy for the sixth time in seven years. But during the Stanley Cup playoffs, he suddenly quit the Canadiens. He just couldn't take it any more and he felt he had to walk out before the game got the best of him.

In 1964 Durnan was elected to Hockey's Hall of Fame. It was a fitting conclusion to his unlikely story. The man who had never played major league hockey until he was 28 years old had one more credit to add to his already amazing record.

CONN SMYTHE'S LUCK

The word *luck* means "that which happens by chance, fortune or lot." By definition, luck can't be controlled—either a person is lucky or he isn't. But some people believe that a man can "make" his own luck. Such a man was Conn Smythe, who became the owner of the Toronto Maple Leafs and one of hockey's great personalities.

During World War I, Smythe was a young officer attached to Canada's 40th Battery. To encourage men to enlist in the army, the Battery organized a hockey team and entered it in the Senior Series of the Ontario Hockey Association. Although Smythe was not much of a hockey player himself, he had great "hockey sense." Because of his skill at judging hockey talent, he became the manager of the 40th Battery team.

Yet Smythe was new to managing, and when the teams got together to draw up the schedule, his rival managers took advantage of him. The first games of the season, played right after Christmas, usually drew the smallest crowds. Without telling him this, the managers convinced Smythe to schedule his first four games on home ice. They figured that he would draw small crowds and lose money. Then, later in the season, when attendance was high, Smythe and the 40th Battery would be playing away from home and the other teams would collect the profits.

But it didn't turn out that way at all. First, all of Smythe's home games were sold out and the 40th

Dapper Conn Smythe, dressed for the opening game of the season, emerges from the Maple Leaf dressing room.

Battery's treasury prospered. Shortly before the fourth game, the battery received orders for shipment overseas. The crafty league managers were to be left in the lurch without a team to play later in the season. So Conn Smythe won and the other league managers lost.

Knowing that the fourth game of the season, against the tough Toronto Argonauts, would be the battery's last, Smythe asked the paymaster how much money was in the team's account.

"About seven thousand dollars," the paymaster said.

Smythe decided to press his luck. He got in touch with a notorious gambler, and secretly bet the team's entire bank account (and the gate receipts of the last game) on his team. Just before the game Smythe told the players what he had done. Some of them may have been shocked at his daring, but they rose to the occasion and slaughtered the Argonauts. Quinn Butterfield, one of the 40th Battery stars, scored five goals in the first eight minutes.

The 40th Battery must have been the richest unit ever to go to war. The league's rival managers had lost, and the gamblers lost. But Conn Smythe and his team won big.

When Smythe returned to Canada after the war was over, he looked for a job in big league hockey. Finally he got his chance in 1926. Colonel John S. Hammond, a rich New York sportsman, had obtained a franchise in the National Hockey League. In order to put together a new team he needed a hockey expert.

Hammond's friend Charles Adams, who owned the Boston Bruins, suggested Conn Smythe. "He's the best judge of hockey players I've ever seen," Adams said. Hammond promptly hired Smythe.

Smythe had plenty of money at his disposal, but he chose carefully. From Port Arthur he got goalie Lorne Chabot. Minneapolis of the Central League yielded two of the greatest defensemen ever to play hockey—Ching Johnson and Taffy Abel. Searching the backwoods of Canada, Smythe came up with brothers Bill and Bun Cook, center Frankie Boucher and reserve center Murray Murdoch. He got the team for $32,000, although experts estimated that the line-up was worth more than $250,000.

Just when it seemed that Smythe was headed for success, Lady Luck's smile turned to a frown. Advisers persuaded Colonel Hammond that Smythe was too inexperienced to manage a major league team. Madison Square Garden, the Rangers' home ice, was a "showplace," they said, and Smythe was not a showman. Hammond agreed. He fired Smythe and hired Lester Patrick. "Lucky" Conn Smythe was left without a job—and he received only $7,500 for his services to the Rangers.

Conn Smythe was determined to get into major league hockey. His eye soon fell on the Toronto St.

Patricks. The Toronto team had fallen on hard times and was up for sale. The problem was that Smythe didn't have enough money even for a down payment. However, he did have three other things: courage, luck and a horse named Rare Jewel.

The two-year-old thoroughbred seemed to be a born loser. Smythe raced the filly five times, and in each race Rare Jewel finished dead last. Before the sixth race, Smythe saw his friend Jack McIntyre, who also owned a hopeless horse. Smythe bet that Rare Jewel would finish last; McIntyre took the bet. Unfortunately, McIntyre's horse was worse than Smythe's—poor Rare Jewel finished next-to-last and Conn lost the bet.

"Even when I pick that nag to lose she can't do it. What a miserable horse!" mourned Smythe. Lady Luck was still frowning.

Smythe took the horse home to Toronto and placed her in the care of a veteran jockey-trainer named Dude Foden. Foden believed that this horse could win if handled properly. The test would come in the Coronation Stakes, a race in which Rare Jewel had been entered before she was born.

In the test before the race Rare Jewel seemed to be flying. "She's ready now," Foden told Smythe jubilantly.

Although some good horses were entered against Rare Jewel, Smythe took the trainer's word. He put down large bets on his horse to win, to place (finish

second) and to show (finish third).

For most of the race Rare Jewel was back in the pack. Then in the home stretch she came to life. Her hooves barely touching the ground, Rare Jewel finished first. Smythe won handsomely. For each $2, he received $219 on his win bet, $49 on his place bet and $18 on his show bet.

Smythe followed up his good fortune by betting his winnings on a couple of hockey games. He won again and had almost enough for a down payment on the Toronto St. Pats. He convinced the sellers to take a little less than they were asking and the team was his. He changed the team name from the St. Patricks to the Maple Leafs (after Canada's national emblem). A few years later he built Maple Leaf Gardens and was soon running one of hockey's most successful franchises.

Was Conn Smythe "just lucky"? Or did he make his own luck? It's hard to be certain. But one thing is sure. Smythe was a born gambler, taking risks that would horrify a timid man. At the very least, Smythe gave Lady Luck plenty of chances.

THE BANANA BLADE

Speed has been one of the pet subjects of sports publicity men. In the late 1930s a 17-year-old pitcher
named Bob Feller joined the Cleveland Indians. Feller's fastball was an eye-blinking, smoke-streaking
blazer. People wondered just how fast it was. By
using a complicated measuring device, the Cleveland publicity men discovered Feller's high hard one
traveled just under 100 miles an hour.

Years later hockey fans were marveling at the
speed of Bobby Hull's slap shot. Once again the
measuring apparatus was set up. It was determined
that Hull's shot zoomed through the air at 110 miles
per hour—and NHL goalies swore that it moved
much faster.

Everybody agreed that Hull had the hardest shot
in hockey. He also became the biggest scorer in the
game.

But actually, Bobby had help—from the "banana
blade."

This strange hockey stick was the result of an accident during the 1960–61 season. As Stan Mikita of
the Chicago Black Hawks skated onto the ice for
practice, he checked his stick and found that the
blade was cracked and bent. Since it was only practice, Mikita decided not to change his stick. He soon
noticed, however, that his passes and shots were act-
ing strangely. The puck seemed to leap off his stick,
often dipping, sailing, dropping or curving.

After practice Hull and a few other Black Hawks

Bobby Hull looks down the curved blade of his stick.

tried the defective stick and got the same results. The secret was all in the curved stick.

Good hockey sticks are expensive, and nobody wanted to crack a few sticks just to see what would happen. Besides, in a game the stick might splinter. But anybody could bend a stick. Several players tried it by shoving the blade under a door, bending it and leaving it in that position overnight.

The results were almost magical. In the next seven years Bobby Hull and Stan Mikita combined to win the scoring championship six times using the banana blade. During the 1968–69 season, Hull fired in 58 goals, which was then the record.

But the banana blade was not to last. The danger to goalies was obvious. Goalie Ed Giacomin declared, "It's hard enough to stop the straight shots, let alone some of those crazy ones. You never know what to expect."

Even some of the forwards using the curved blades were dissatisfied. Some players using sticks with deeply curved blades found that they had trouble controlling the puck on fast dashes down the ice. Also their passes were less accurate. And it was almost impossible to get off a backhand shot. Even the shooter didn't know where the puck would go.

The rules of all sports are set up to keep a good

Despite the outlawing of the banana blade, Phil Esposito scored 76 goals in 1970–71.

balance between offense and defense. Hockey rule-makers realized that the banana blade was putting too much pressure on the defense and giving the offense too much of an advantage. Thus they began to reduce the amount of curve allowed in a hockey stick. In the 1968–69 season the maximum curve, or "bow," permitted was one and a half inches. The next year the maximum was reduced to one inch, and then down to a half-inch.

Some fans sourly said that it was goodbye to the high scorers. They felt that much of hockey's excitement would be lost because of the new limitations. Oddly enough it didn't work out that way at all.

When Phil Esposito was with the Black Hawks, one of his heroes was Bobby Hull. Esposito watched Hull closely and noticed the curved sticks he was then using. During one practice session Phil borrowed one of Bobby's sticks and immediately liked the feel of the curved blade.

Esposito had been traded to Boston by the time the new rules limiting curved blades were passed. He was one of many who felt the rules would hurt the scorers. How wrong he was!

In the 1970–71 season, using a stick with only a half-inch curve in the blade, Phil Esposito broke every NHL scoring record. He racked up 76 goals and 76 assists, for a grand total of 152 points. Banana blades were out, but scoring was higher than ever!

HOCKEY'S WORST FIGHT

Professional athletes are naturally competitive. It is their job to play hard and well, and more often than not they are keyed-up and tense even for an unimportant game. It is not surprising that in almost every professional sport there is an occasional fight between two or more players. When a player is shoved or hit in a scramble for a loose ball, for example, he may lose his temper and let fly with a few punches. Most of the time the battle is over in a couple of seconds, when cooler heads prevail and the fighters are separated.

It's a little different in hockey. Hockey is famous for long, ferocious fights that sometimes involve both teams and the fans as well. Some famous brawls have lasted a quarter of an hour before order could be restored. In at least one case, a woman fan accosted a player with her handbag.

Strangely enough, the worst fight in hockey history lasted only a few seconds and consisted of one shove and one punch. Only three players were involved. But the result was a near-tragedy.

The fight occurred on December 12, 1933, in a game between the Boston Bruins and the Toronto Maple Leafs. At the center of the dispute was Eddie Shore of the Bruins. Shore was one of the greatest defensemen in hockey. He was also a rough-and-tumble player, famous for his savage checks and competitive drive.

Supposedly, Eddie had tried to "play like a gentleman" the early part of the season, but he found it didn't pay. Before the Toronto game he told a sportswriter that he was ready to return to the rock-'em, sock-'em style of hockey that players and fans had come to expect of him.

In the first period Toronto scored a goal. Moments later, the Leafs suffered two penalties that sent Andy Blair and Hap Day to the penalty box. Forced to play two men short, Toronto coach Dick Irvin sent in his penalty-killers—Red Horner and the great King Clancy on defense, and Ace Bailey at forward, a marvelous stickhandler and skater. Their job was to keep the puck away from the Bruins until the penalty time had elapsed.

Bailey got possession of the puck and skillfully avoided the rush by Boston. He kept dodging, twisting, slowing and speeding, but he was not advancing the puck as the rules say you must. So the referee whistled for a face-off. Bailey quickly regained possession, and after using up a few more seconds, he sent the puck sailing across the ice into Boston territory.

Eddie Shore intercepted the black disc and stormed up the ice. King Clancy, another great defenseman, moved in on Shore and knocked him off balance. Shore fell to his knees near the blue line, skidded a few feet and came to rest near the boards. He remained there briefly, catching his breath. Shore later claimed he was dazed by the vicious

Eddie Shore works out with the New York Americans late in his career.

check Clancy had given him.

When Shore climbed to his feet he was an angry man. No one had done anything illegal to him, but he was out to hit somebody. A Leaf player was across the ice, his back to Eddie. Perhaps Shore thought it was King Clancy, the man who had shoved him out of the play. Actually, it was Ace Bailey.

Shore dug into the ice, gained speed and rammed into Bailey at full speed, flipping the Toronto forward high into the air. Bailey smashed to the ice with a horrifying thud and lay motionless, his neck at a strange angle. Instantly the crowd at Boston fell silent. They sensed immediately that Bailey had been seriously injured.

Red Horner went to his fallen teammate's side, knelt near him for a moment, then got to his feet and skated over to Shore.

"Why did you do that, Eddie?" he demanded.

Shore did not know how badly Bailey had been hurt. Horner said that instead of replying, Shore smiled thinly. Red flew into a blind rage. Bracing his feet, he landed a thundering uppercut on Shore's chin. The Boston defenseman fell backward, his head hitting the ice. Almost immediately the ice was stained red by Shore's blood.

Strangely, that was the end of the fighting. Somehow, people seemed to know that Shore would be all right—nothing could really hurt that rugged man.

But Ace Bailey was in trouble.

Bailey was rushed to a hospital. Doctors did not immediately know how badly he was hurt, but eventually they announced that he had suffered a double fracture of the skull. They listed Bailey in critical condition and did not give him much of a chance to pull through.

The finest specialists and surgeons in Boston fought hard to save Ace Bailey's life. Newspapers and radio stations carried bulletins of the operations performed on Bailey, and they told how the nurses stayed at his bedside night and day. Everyone was pulling for him to make it. And eventually he did, although he was never to play hockey again.

On February 14, 1934, only two months later, Bailey had recovered enough to attend an "Ace Bailey Benefit Night" in Maple Leaf Gardens. The Leafs were playing an NHL All-Star team that night, and Eddie Shore was one of the all-stars.

Before the game the opposing teams lined up along the blue line. Ace Bailey walked slowly toward the center of the ice, and the sell-out crowd of 15,000 fans grew tense. What would happen when Bailey and Shore faced each other?

They soon found out. Eddie Shore left his place in the all-star ranks and skated over toward Bailey with hand outstretched. Bailey grasped Shore's hand in forgiveness and the two stars embraced each other. The fans cheered so loudly the rink trembled.

Ace Bailey (left) shakes hands with Eddie Shore several months after the incident that ended Bailey's hockey career.

Eddie Shore had been criticized by newspapers and booed by fans after the Ace Bailey incident. But sports fans seldom hold grudges. Eddie Shore played his usual rough hockey that night in Toronto. He pressed his opponents recklessly, never backing down. Among those cheering him on were the Toronto fans—and Ace Bailey.

UNSUNG HERO

One of hockey's most famous stories is about a team that lost its goalie in a Stanley Cup playoff. In 1928 New York Ranger coach Lester Patrick stepped into the goal crease to fill in for the regular goalie, who had been injured. Although Patrick was 45 years old, he allowed only one goal and the Rangers won the game 2-1.

Yet very few people remember the story of another last-minute substitute whose performance was as good. His name was Alfie Moore and he played for the 1938 Chicago Black Hawks.

The Black Hawks were a strange team that year. The coach, "Bald Bill" Stewart, was a former major league baseball umpire. During the regular season the team won only 14 games, but they did manage to squeak into the Stanley Cup playoffs.

Chicago surprised even their own fans by winning the semifinal series over Montreal. Next they were to face the Toronto Maple Leafs in the finals. The Leafs were a powerhouse team and they were heavily favored over the Hawks.

Before the first game was played, things started to go wrong for the lowly Hawks. Their goalie, Mike Karakas, had broken a toe, and on the day of the first game it was so swollen that he couldn't fit his foot into his skate. The Hawks requested permission to use Dave Kerr of the New York Rangers as a replacement. But Conn Smythe, the crafty owner of the Maple Leafs, knew his rights and refused permission.

The Hawks desperately tried to find somebody—*anybody*—who could fill in. Finally, at the last minute, they found Alfie Moore.

Hockey coach-baseball umpire Bill Stewart (left) admires the Stanley Cup with two of his Black Hawk players.

Alfie had been guarding the nets for the minor league Pittsburgh club. He had tried out for the majors but just wasn't good enough. Although he had never played in an NHL game, suddenly he was in the Stanley Cup finals, where the pressure was terrific and the stakes were high.

Maybe the Black Hawks played harder because they realized an inexperienced goalie was in the net. Or maybe Alfie simply played above his ability for that one game. Whatever the reason, the minor league goalie took the best the Leafs could throw at him. He permitted only one goal while Chicago scored three times to win.

After the game Stewart asked Moore how much he wanted to be paid.

"I don't know," murmured Alfie. "Would a hundred and fifty be too much?"

The Hawks gave him $300 for his night's work, plus an inscribed gold watch.

The league ruled Alfie ineligible after that one game, so a goalie from a Chicago farm team, Paul Goodman, played in the next match. Unfortunately, Toronto knocked him around and won 5-1.

Mike Karakas came back for the remaining games, and the Hawks took the Cup by winning the final two games of the series. It was a great upset and unknown Alfie Moore had played his part in it.

When Lester Patrick saved a playoff game for his team, he was an old man by hockey standards. Yet he had been one of the great defensive players in the history of the game. Alfie Moore was not even a major leaguer. He had his moment of glory and then faded from the scene. But for that one game he was superb and he too earned a place in the history of hockey.

BROTHERS

The pass was wide of the mark. The puck bounced off the boards and skidded behind the net. Chasing it were two players on the same team, one a wingman the other a center. So eager were they to gain possession of the elusive disc that neither man noticed the other. They banged together with a shuddering crash and fell to the ice. The wingman needed twelve stitches to close his cuts; the center required six.

Later, as they were being patched up in the dressing room, the wingman muttered through bruised lips, "Be careful little brother. You're liable to get hurt."

The wingman was Rocket Richard; the center was his younger brother, Henri, whom people called "The Pocket Rocket."

Hockey has a long history of "brother acts." There are brothers in all sports, but more in hockey than in any other game. In fact the very history of hockey could almost be written in stories about brothers.

When hockey was just beginning as a professional sport, two brothers came along who contributed more to the game's development than any other two men. According to one story, Lester Patrick wrote hockey's first rule book. His brother Frank corrected it. Together the Patricks founded the Pacific Coast

Muzz (left) and Lester Patrick, members of "hockey's royal family," in 1942.

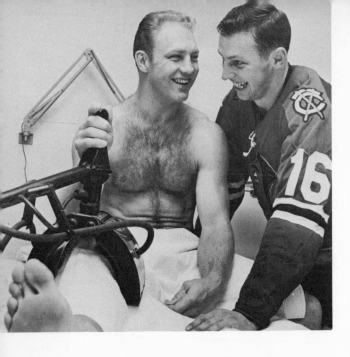

Three of hockey's great brother combinations: Bobby and Dennis Hull (top), Maurice and Henri Richard (bottom), and Tony and Phil Esposito (right).

League in 1912 and during their long careers as players, coaches and managers, they helped the game spread across Canada and into the United States. Lester spent many years as manager of the New York Rangers, beginning in 1927. Two of his sons, Lynn and Murray "Muzz" Patrick, became another "brother act," playing for the Rangers and becoming hockey executives. The four Patricks became known as "Hockey's Royal Family."

What happens when brothers play against each other? Do they take it easy, do they pull their punches? Hardly! In a hockey game it's the team that counts, not relatives.

In the 1930s, Lionel "Big Train" Conacher played for the Montreal Maroons, while his younger brother, Charlie, skated with the Toronto Maple Leafs. During one game between the two teams a fight started between Toronto's Red Horner and Montreal's Gus Marker. They were pulled apart and sent to cool off in the penalty box. As Horner passed the Montreal bench he spoke some sharp words to Lionel Conacher. Lionel swung at Horner. Charlie Conacher came over to separate his teammate from his brother. But when he was unsuccessful, he slugged his brother in the face. Nor did he let matters rest there. Later in the game Charlie got back. He took a swipe at the puck, aiming it at Lionel, and hit him in the ankle. Lionel retaliated by checking Charlie with a hard block that knocked him to the ice. After the game was over, Charlie was quoted as saying, "Nobody hits a member of the Maple Leafs —not even my brother!"

Years after the Conachers, Tony Esposito began to tend goal for the Chicago Black Hawks. He had to face his brother Phil in his very first game. Phil had no mercy. He turned the hat trick, scoring three goals. But after the game one of Phil's Boston team-mates questioned Tony's ability as a net-minder. Suddenly Phil was Tony's brother again. He told his teammate to shut up.

Many of the famous hockey brothers have played on the same team. Maurice and Henri Richard and Bobby and Dennis Hull spent much of their careers playing together. One of the great brother combina-tions was Max and Doug Bentley. Opponents soon learned to respect both their performance and their teamwork.

There were thirteen Bentley kids. Max was the youngest and one of the smallest (even as an NHL star he weighed less than 150 pounds). He was also the best all-around athlete.

Sometimes several of the Bentleys would play to-gether. Once in a baseball game, Max, who was the best hitter, got a base hit. Suddenly five of the Bentleys huddled with Max at first base. When the huddle broke, no one on the other team could tell which brother was Max—they all looked more or less alike. One of the Bentleys—nobody seemed to

The Bentley brothers: Reggie, Max and Doug.

know which one—stayed on first base while another Bentley took a turn at bat. Opponents suspected that Max was batting again, but nobody could prove it.

Max and brother Doug starred for the Chicago Black Hawks during the 1940s, and both were among the greatest scorers in the game. Unlike many brothers their records were almost identical. Sometimes it seemed that if one brother did something noteworthy, the other brother had to match it immediately.

In a 1943 game against the Rangers, the Bentleys scored five goals in the third period. Max scored four goals and Doug one. But Doug had an assist on each of Max's goals. That year Doug led the NHL in points scored. The next season he had the most goals but not the most points. Max brought the scoring leadership back to the family by leading the league in 1946 and 1947.

Late in their careers the Bentleys were separated when Max was traded to the Toronto Maple Leafs. Although they continued to play great hockey, somehow the old fire seemed to be lacking.

Then in 1954 the brothers were reunited. Doug went to the Rangers and Max was coaxed out of retirement to join Doug for one more year on the ice together. In their first game as a team each brother had a pair of goals and each had three assists!

The final totals of the Bentley brothers were remarkably similar. In 12 NHL seasons Max scored 241 goals and 544 points. In 13 seasons Doug had 220 goals and 543 points.

Down through the years hockey has had an incredible number of brothers in competition; indeed, there were so many that it is all but impossible to mention them all. But teammates or opponents, the great brother combinations of hockey have made it the top "family" game.

SISTER COACH

A passerby stopped for a few moments at an outdoor rink to watch some young hockey players go through a lively scrimmage. The boys were between the ages of 10 and 14, and some of them had surprisingly good form. They skated and passed pretty well.

One of the youngsters drove a hard shot toward the net. Bobby York, the 13-year-old goalie, fell to his knees and smothered the puck. Then a whistle blew at the other end of the rink. The kids skated slowly off the ice toward a dark-clothed figure.

The spectator was filled with admiration for the style shown by the young goalie. "Hey, where'd you learn to play like that?" he called out.

"Mostly by practicing hard," said Bobby, smiling.

"Didn't your coach give you a few tips?"

"Oh, sure. But she also figures we're smart enough to learn a thing or two by ourselves."

"*She?*" The man was dumfounded. Bobby pointed across the rink, and now the man could see that the dark-clothed figure was a nun!

"That's our coach," Bobby said with a grin.

"Since when?" asked the man, staring doubtfully at the tall figure in the black robe and white pointed headdress.

"As long as I can remember," Bobby said. "Sister St. Barbara Ann is the principal of our Queen of the Angels School. She also teaches us math and coaches our other athletic teams." Then he skated away.

Sister St. Barbara Ann had become an athletic

coach by accident. She had always been fond of sports. Before entering the convent her favorites were skiing and skating. Although she hadn't played much hockey, she was an avid fan and watched many games on television.

After she took her vows, Sister St. Barbara Ann taught at Notre Dame High School in Toronto and at St. Patrick's High School in Ottawa. Later she became principal of Queen of the Angels School in Ottawa. She believed that sports were as important for youngsters as math, history and reading. Not only did the competition keep them out of mischief, but it also helped build their bodies.

Since Queen of the Angels School was operated by an order of nuns, there were no men to coach the athletic teams. Sister St. Barbara Ann assumed the job herself. If some of the boys didn't like the idea of a nun coaching a hockey team, they soon found out that Sister St. Barbara Ann was nobody to trifle with. She knew the fundamentals of every position from studying the styles of such players as Gordie Howe and Bobby Hull on television. She also sketched out a few good basic plays.

Sister St. Barbara Ann insisted that every boy in school who wanted to play be given a chance. She didn't approve of letting only the best players participate. Thus there was also an intramural league, in which all teams were made up of Queen of the Angels students.

The wise nun made the boys understand that sportsmanship and fair play were more important than winning a game. "We do like to win," she said, smiling slightly, "but it isn't everything. Being a good person—*that* is everything."

Sister St. Barbara Ann had to overcome many obstacles to keep the team going. The school's budget did not permit renting a rink for practice, so the team had to work out at a local rink which contributed free time. However, others also wanted to use the rink, so the Queen of the Angels team couldn't always practice as much as they wanted to. Still, they managed to do fairly well in competition.

Sometimes the boys at Queen of the Angels were teased about their coach. After all, hockey is usually a game for men. How did they feel about being taught and managed by a woman?

All the boys were quick to defend Sister St. Barbara Ann. They pointed out that she was a student of sports, that she had studied positions and plays. She also permitted the boys to make suggestions and, if anyone had a good play to try out, Sister St. Barbara Ann always let him test it.

The results of all their group work were often quite encouraging. One year the Queen of the Angels hockey team got into the league semi-finals before being eliminated. And a few seasons ago the touch football team won the league gold cup!

What the boys enjoyed most about their principal-teacher-coach was that she was also their loudest cheerleader. They thought it was marvelous when she shouted out at a game—"Go, Go, Queen of the Angels! Go, Go!"

THE OVERTIME SCORERS

For most people, the most exciting part of hockey is the overtime game. Overtimes are played only in Stanley Cup competition when the score is tied at the end of regulation time. The first team to score is the winner and a "sudden death" goal is one of the great contributions a player can make to his team. Hockey's championship, the Stanley Cup, is at stake whenever a "sudden death" goal is scored.

More often than not the winning goal in an overtime game is scored by a great star who comes through in the clutch. In a 1928 overtime game between the New York Rangers and the Montreal Maroons, it was Frankie Boucher, the great Ranger center, who put the game away with a solo dash down the ice. In the first game of the 1951 Canadiens–Red Wings playoffs, the winning goal was scored by Rocket Richard after 61 minutes and 9 seconds of extra play. Some of the great overtime goals, however, have been scored by players who would otherwise be unknown. They were not stars or high scorers. But because of their goals in one or two crucial situations, their names have become a part of hockey legend.

In the first game of the 1936 playoffs between Detroit and the Montreal Maroons, the teams played all-out hockey. At the end of regulation time, the score was deadlocked 0-0. In the first overtime the teams tore into each other again, but there were no scores. A second overtime passed and then a third.

After an extra hour of hard play, both nets remained undented.

The players were dog tired, but the game went on and on. Overtime periods four and five passed into history. Both goalies made fantastic saves and it was still a zero-score hockey game.

The sixth overtime was almost over when Detroit's Hec Kilrea picked up the puck and skated toward the Montreal goal. At his side was Moderre "Mud" Bruneteau. Kilrea faked as Bruneteau moved around the net. When Montreal goalie Chabot came out to meet the threat, Kilrea passed to Bruneteau, who fired into the open net. The Red Wings had won after 2 hours, 56 minutes and 30 seconds. It was easily the longest game on record (it ended at 2:20 in the morning).

Mud Bruneteau was a rookie with the Red Wings. He spent most of the 1935–36 season with a Detroit farm team. During his time with the Red Wings, he had scored only two goals. Yet his goal ended hockey's longest game and Detroit went on to win the Stanley Cup.

The 1939 playoffs provided another strange chapter for fans who love overtime games. The Boston Bruins faced the New York Rangers and in the first game the score was tied at 1-all in regulation time. Two overtime periods left the score tied. Near the end of the third extra period, a Boston player named Mel Hill poked the puck into the net. He scored

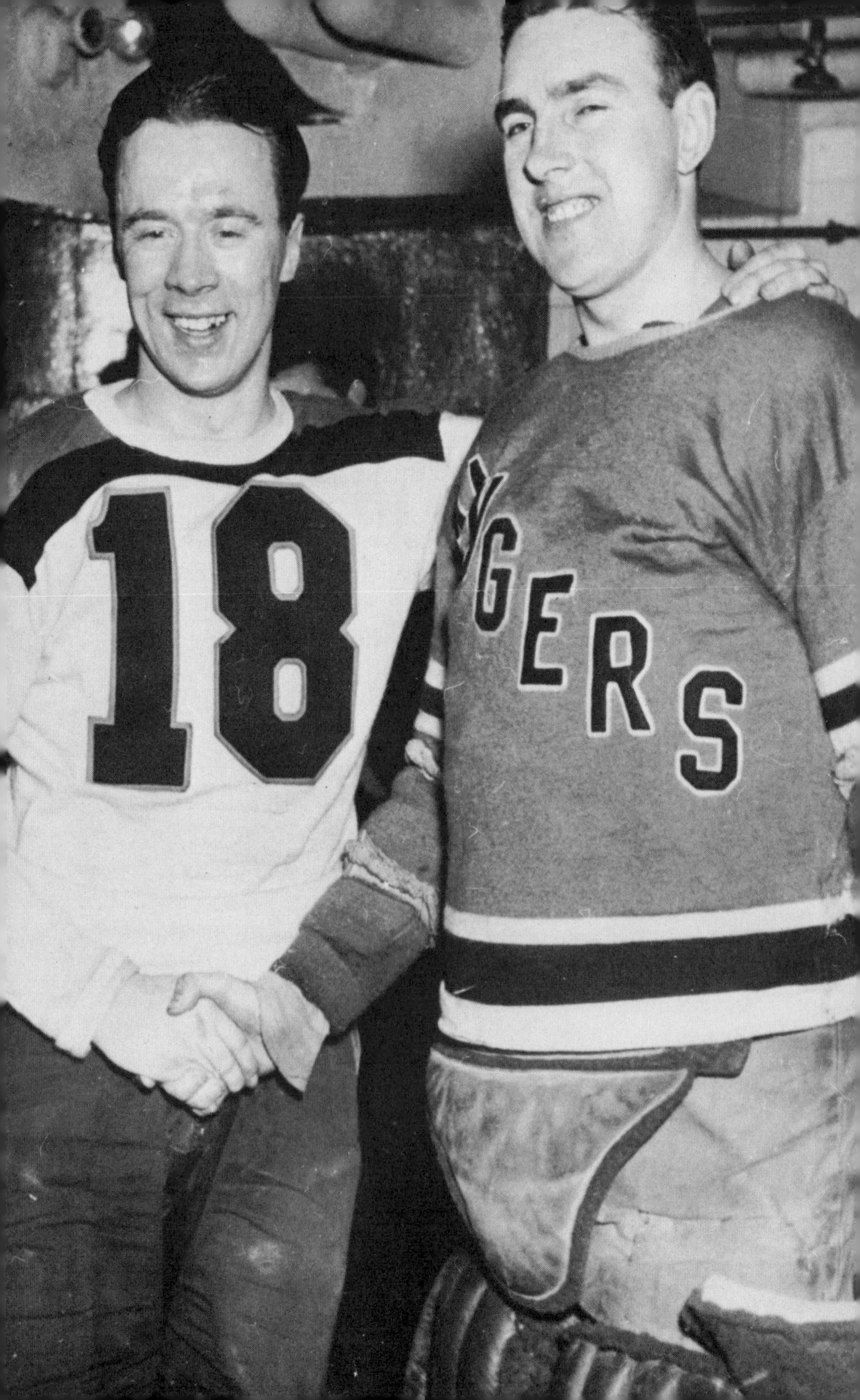
18
GERS

after 59 minutes and 25 seconds of extra hockey.

The second game of the series was also tied at the end of 60 minutes, this time at 2-all. After 8:24 of the first overtime, the Bruins had the winning goal. The man who zipped in the puck was Mel Hill.

Boston won the third game in regulation time, 4-1, and it seemed that New York was finished. But Lester Patrick's Rangers refused to quit, and they came storming back with three straight victories, one of them in overtime.

The seventh game would decide the series. At the conclusion of regulation time, the score was tied 1-1. Two overtime periods left the score tied. At the 8-minute mark of the third overtime, Boston finally cracked through to win.

The deciding goal was scored by—Mel Hill!

Three of Boston's victories had been in overtime, and in each of those games Mel Hill had been the hero. Oddly enough, Hill had tried out with the Rangers but couldn't make the team. And he certainly wasn't much of a scorer; in the 1939 regular season he had scored only ten goals. Yet Hill was given the nickname "Sudden Death," and he is remembered wherever people follow hockey.

Mel Hill (left) is congratulated by Ranger goalie Bert Gardiner after Hill scored his third sudden-death goal in the 1939 Stanley Cup finals.

The rarest of all overtime action was the 1951 Stanley Cup finals between the Toronto Maple Leafs and Montreal Canadiens. The series went five games and every one of those games went into overtime!

Game one was taken by Toronto in 5 minutes and 51 seconds of the first overtime period on a goal by Sid Smith.

The second contest was won by Montreal at the 2:55 overtime mark when Rocket Richard got through to score.

In the third contest, tough Ted Kennedy, one of hockey's finest players, cracked one in after 4 minutes and 47 seconds of extra hockey. Toronto led in the series two games to one.

The fourth game was also won by Toronto on Harry Watson's goal at 5:15 of the first overtime.

Montreal was leading 2-1 in the fifth game with only one minute to play. Maple Leaf coach Joe Primeau pulled his goalie and sent a sixth attacker onto the ice, hoping to gain a tie. With 32 seconds left, Tod Sloan scored for Toronto. The score was tied 2-2 and the fifth game in a row went into overtime.

At 2:53 of the overtime, a rugged defenseman named Bill Barilko took a pass from teammate Howie Meeker, crossed the blue line and took a wild shot. The puck skidded past Montreal goalie Gerry McNeil and into the net. Toronto had won the Stanley Cup.

What kind of player scored the winning goal? Barilko was a fine defenseman, but in his best NHL season he scored just seven goals!

There is a sad footnote to the story. That Stanley Cup goal was the final marker of Bill Barilko's life. In August of that year he went on a fishing trip with a friend named Henry Hudson, in Hudson's airplane. The plane never reached its destination. Fifteen years later, parts of the wreckage were discovered, but the bodies of the two men were never found.

It's true, there's nothing more exciting than overtime hockey. And sometimes the winning goals are scored by the unlikeliest players.

SPORTSMANSHIP

Every four years the nations of the world send their finest young athletes—men and women—to the Olympic Games. People of all races and beliefs have a common bond at these Games—the friendly competition of sports.

The Olympic symbol is designed to point out the basic brotherhood of man. The five linked circles of this symbol represent the friendship of the continents: Asia, Africa, North and South America, Europe and Australia. The Olympic colors are blue, yellow, black, green and red, because at least one of these colors appears in the flag of every nation in the world. The Olympic motto—*Citius, Altius, Fortius* —means "Swifter, Higher, Stronger."

Baron Pierre de Coubertin founded the modern Olympic Games in 1896 and wrote the Olympic Creed: "The most important thing in the Olympic Games is not to win but to take part, just as the most important thing in life is not the triumph but the struggle. The essential thing is not to have conquered but to have fought well."

But do the participating nations really believe in the meaning of these Olympic contests? Most of them do. But unfortunately, some nations have tried to use their victories as proof that they are better than the rest of the world.

In 1936 Germany hosted the Olympic Games. That year a black American athlete named Jesse Owens impressed the world with his fantastic accomplishments in track and field. But when he received his gold medals, Nazi dictator Adolph Hitler refused to congratulate him. Hitler had boasted that his fair-haired, blue-eyed "Aryan" athletes were the best in the world, and he refused to admit that his finest sprinters and jumpers had lost to a Negro.

The Olympic athletes themselves, however, have often had a spirit of fair play and true sportsmanship that governments have lacked. Perhaps the story of the 1960 Olympic Hockey Games illustrates this point.

In the early years of the Olympics, the hockey event was dominated by Canada and the United States. But the United States grew weaker over the years, mainly because hockey was less important than football, track and basketball in the colleges—there were simply fewer good players to choose from. At the same time Russian teams were getting better, and soon they were the team to beat.

The 1960 American Olympic hockey team did not seem particularly strong. The players, all amateurs, were pretty good, but no one seemed particularly outstanding.

The team captain was John Kirrane, a defenseman from Brookline, Massachusetts. Kirrane was 29 then —the "old man" of the team. He had taken part in the 1948 Olympics when he was only 17. Playing alongside him was John Mayasich, a former all-American from the University of Minnesota.

The team also included Bill Cleary, a former Harvard hockey player, and his brother, Bob; Bill Christian, a Minnesota all-American, and his brother, Roger, who made his living as a carpenter; Paul Johnson, another Minnesota player; Weldon Olson of Marquette, who had played in the 1956 Olympics; and Bob Owen. The team's head coach was Jack Riley, the coach at West Point.

For a while the team had no goalie. Coach Riley had tried out two players from the East and both were disappointing. Finally he heard about Jack McCarten, a private in the U.S. Army stationed at Fort Carson, Colorado. Riley looked McCarten over, and chose him as his first-string goalie.

None of these players were professional athletes (pros are not permitted to compete in the Olympics). They played simply out of love for the sport. To the experts they seemed like a funny collection: two insurance salesmen, a television advertising man, a fireman, a carpenter, a soldier, and other assorted citizens. Eight of the players had never engaged in international competition. Few people expected them to be serious contenders.

The games were being played at Squaw Valley, California. In its first match, the United States team proved that it wasn't a pushover. It was losing to Czechoslovakia 4-3 when Paul Johnson took a pass and scored the tying goal. Then Johnny Mayasich got the go-ahead goal (his third of the

Bill Christian (6) of the U.S. knocks down the Soviet Union's Nikolai Sologu-bov in the 1960 Olympics.

game) with a long shot from the blue line. Tom Williams and Bill Cleary each added a goal and the Americans won 7-5.

That come-from-behind victory was followed by a convincing 12-1 win over the willing but inexperienced Australian team. The Americans didn't gloat over it though, for the day before the Czechs had beaten Australia 18-1. Still, the win put the U.S. into the championship series with Sweden, Germany, Canada, Russia and Czechoslovakia.

The U.S. club beat Sweden next. The Swedish team was hobbled by injuries, but still the Americans proved they were sharp. Roger Christian scored a hat trick (three goals) and his brother got three assists. Bob Cleary, McVey and Johnson also scored.

Next the U.S. squad routed Germany 9-1. Then came the tough Canadians. America's northern neighbors were excellent hockey players and they figured to win. The Americans drew first blood, however, when Bob Cleary picked up a rebound from the stick of the Canadian goalie and poked it into the net. Later, Paul Johnson intercepted a pass, dodged down the ice and scored with a backhand shot. Back came the aroused Canadians. But McCarten, the American goalie, was spectacular, blocking shot after shot. Finally, with 14:38 gone in the third period, the Canadians scored. But after that goalie McCarten bolted the door and the Americans won 2-1.

The Russians were next, and few tougher or faster games of hockey have been seen since. The game seesawed back and forth. First the Americans took the lead, then the Russians tied. A few minutes later the Russians scored again and went ahead. Later on, the Americans tied it up once more.

The score was 2-2 when the game went into the final period. McCarten was playing a strong game in the nets. The Russians were sending a steady barrage of shots his way, but he was stopping them cold. McCarten had been a last-minute addition to the team, but now he was becoming its hero.

At 14:59 Billy Christian scored the final goal of the game. The Americans had upset the Russians 3-2!

The United States had one more game to play—against Czechoslovakia—and they needed a win to assure a gold medal.

The Americans had defeated the Czechs before, but after two periods of this last game they had run out of steam. They were losing 4-3.

As they sat dejectedly in the dressing room before the last period, they were visited by a Russian player named Nikolai Sologubov. Solly, as the Americans called him, had been friendly with some of the American players. He suggested that they breathe some pure oxygen to regain their strength. Squaw Valley was a mile above sea level and the thin air had little oxygen, exhausting athletes who were used

to lower altitudes.

Solly pointed out that there was no rule against using oxygen. The Russians themselves had used it freely and no one had complained.

A number of the Americans inhaled oxygen and felt better. But even those who didn't use the oxygen were inspired by Solly's sportsmanlike gesture.

The Americans swarmed all over the startled Czechs in the third period. Bob and Bill Cleary and Roger Christian together scored three goals in 67 seconds. Roger Christian scored four goals altogether in the game. The Americans scored six goals in the final period to overwhelm Czechoslovakia 9-4. The United States had won the gold medal in hockey!

Long after the Olympic Games were over, coaches and athletes around the world talked of "Solly" Sologubov's action. Why had he told the Americans about oxygen?

Was it because he did not want Czechoslovakia to win? He may have felt that it would be a disgrace to have a small communist nation finish ahead of the Soviet Union. But most people felt that Solly acted as a true sportsman, seeking to help the underdogs

Sologubov and U.S. coach Jack Riley congratulate each other after the U.S. team beat Czechoslovakia to win the gold medal.

The jubilant U.S. team poses for a picture after their victory.

by giving them advice in the spirit of Olympic comradeship.

Even if nations sometimes forgot the ideals of the Olympic Games, it seemed that the athletes themselves often remembered and lived up to them.

INDEX

Page numbers in italics refer to photographs

About the Author

Howard Liss has written many books for children, including *The Making of a Rookie, Baseball's Zaniest Stars, More Strange But True Baseball Stories* and *Strange But True Basketball Stories.* He has also collaborated on books with such sports stars as Yogi Berra, Willie Mays and Y. A. Tittle. Mr. Liss lives in New York City.